**FEDERAL FORCES**

CAREERS AS
FEDERAL AGENTS

# A CAREER AS A
# DEA AGENT

**DAWN RAPINE**

**PowerKiDS**
press

New York

Published in 2016 by The Rosen Publishing Group, Inc.
29 East 21st Street, New York, NY 10010

First Edition

Editor: Caitlin McAneney
Book Design: Mickey Harmon

Photo Credits: Cover (DEA agent) fstop123/E+/Getty Images; cover (logo) Color Symphony/ Shutterstock.com; cover, pp. 1, 3–32 (mesh texture) Eky Studio/Shutterstock.com; pp. 5, 11 ASSOCIATED PRESS/APImages.com; p. 7 Chicago History Museum/Contributor/Archive Photos/Getty Images; p. 9 (emblem) MANDEL NGAN/Staff/AFP/Getty Images; p. 9 (background) http://en.wikipedia.org/ wiki/Pentagon_City#/media/File:Office_buildings_in_Pentagon_City.JPG; p. 13 Sandy Huffaker/Stringer/ Getty Images News/Getty Images; p. 17 Courtesy of the 134th ARW, Tennessee National Guard; p. 19 Monkey Business Images/Shutterstock.com; p. 21 bikeriderlondon/Shutterstock.com; p. 22 Peter Kim/Shutterstock.com; p. 23 wavebreakmedia/Shutterstock.com; p. 25 MADEL NGAN/AFP/ Getty Images; p. 27 Kathryn Scott Osler/Contributor/Denver Post/Getty Images; p. 29 Ammentorp Photography/Shutterstock.com; p. 30 http://upload.wikimedia.org/wikipedia/commons/8/83/DEA_ badge_C.PNG.

Cataloging-in-Publication Data

Rapine, Dawn.
A career as a DEA agent / by Dawn Rapine.
p. cm. — (Federal forces: careers as federal agents)
Includes index.
ISBN 978-1-4994-1058-7 (pbk.)
ISBN 978-1-4994-1094-5 (6 pack)
ISBN 978-1-4994-1113-3 (library binding)
1. United States. Drug Enforcement Administration — Juvenile literature. 2. Criminal investigation — Vocational guidance — United States — Juvenile literature. 3. Law enforcement — Vocational guidance — United States — Juvenile literature. I. Rapine, Dawn. II. Title.
HV5825.R36 2016
363.25'9770973—d23

Manufactured in the United States of America

CPSIA Compliance Information: Batch #WS15PK: For Further Information contact Rosen Publishing, New York, New York at 1-800-237-9932

# Contents

# What Is the DEA?

All around the world, drugs are being grown or created, processed, brought to new places, and used. It's the job of special agents from the Drug Enforcement Administration (DEA) to track down illegal drug activity wherever it may take place.

The main job of the DEA is to enforce the nation's controlled substance laws. Controlled substances include illegal drugs and legal **prescription** drugs. They also include drugs supplied without a prescription or doctor's instructions. Using drugs often has a negative effect on a person's health and well-being, especially if a doctor hasn't prescribed them. The DEA works to stop people from making, supplying, acquiring, possessing, and using these drugs. People who are involved with illegal drugs could be arrested and sent to prison.

DEA agents work to keep people safe from drugs and violence.

# Before the DEA

Although the DEA was created in 1973, the federal government has been **prosecuting** people who break drug laws and **abuse** drugs since the early 1900s. The Bureau of Internal Revenue (now called the Internal Revenue Service or IRS) was the first agency to enforce drug laws. This is the same agency that collects taxes.

The DEA began as the Bureau of Narcotics and Dangerous Drugs (BNDD), which was formed in 1968. BNDD brought together bureaus from the Department of the Treasury and the Department of Health, Education, and Welfare (now called the Department of Health and Human Services) under one agency in the Department of Justice. In 1973, BNDD added more offices and changed its name to the Drug Enforcement Administration.

From 1920 until 1933, Americans were banned from selling alcohol. This period of time was called Prohibition. The Bureau of Internal Revenue enforced Prohibition, so agents were called "revenuers" by bootleggers who sold alcohol illegally.

# How Does the DEA Do Its Job?

To find people engaged in drug crimes, the DEA needs only the best agents, teams, and resources. Some DEA agents track drug offenders around the country. Others are part of investigative teams that handle cases ranging from small local drug sellers, or dealers, to international drug-**trafficking** rings. Agents and investigators receive **intelligence** reports to help them find and catch suspected criminals. Analysts review controlled-substance usage around the country to see if usage is increasing or decreasing or if new drugs are being introduced. **Forensic** specialists review and test evidence gathered during investigations.

The DEA has 221 offices around the United States. There are also 86 foreign offices in 67 different countries. DEA headquarters are in Arlington County, Virginia, near the Pentagon.

The DEA works with local and state officials in the enforcement of drug laws. They also work with drug enforcement agencies in other countries to reduce the amount of drugs that come into the United States.

# Special Agents

A career as a special agent includes many different kinds of work, which sometimes involve danger. Agents arrest drug traffickers both in the United States and foreign countries. They investigate crimes by interviewing witnesses and collecting evidence involved in drug operations. They analyze and prepare the evidence for prosecuting suspects in court.

Some agents do undercover work. Sometimes they pose as criminals so they can join drug gangs and find out how they work and what illegal operations they're involved with. They may also **impersonate** drug dealers, shippers, or buyers. They may even engage in illegal activity to prove to drug traffickers that they're not law enforcement officers. This is very dangerous work, and special agents who work undercover regularly work in harm's way.

# Marijuana: Legal or Illegal?

Marijuana is a drug consisting of the dried parts of a plant called *Cannabis*. It contains a mind-altering chemical. Marijuana is still illegal according to federal laws. However, many states have legalized the sale or limited possession of marijuana for medical or even personal use. Local and state law enforcement officers in those states can't arrest adults for possessing a limited amount of marijuana. However, DEA agents still enforce federal drug laws throughout the country, including states that have legalized marijuana.

This DEA special agent stands with nearly 600 pounds (272 kg) of marijuana seized in Oklahoma City, Oklahoma.

# Agents Around the World

Many special agents work on overseas assignments. Special agents on the Foreign-Deployed Advisory Support Teams (FAST) program pursue drug growers and producers in countries such as Afghanistan and Mexico. These are difficult operations, sometimes in war zones. Agents often work with the military and local authorities in those countries to complete their assignments.

The special agents who work in international DEA offices **monitor** drug enforcement cases, targeting major drug-trafficking organizations and **money-laundering** networks. They share intelligence with local law enforcement to crack down on these networks. Knowing foreign languages is a plus if you want to work in overseas offices.

Special agents who work along the Mexican border find tunnels used to transfer drugs from Mexico to the United States.

# Operation Boomer/Falcon

The Turks and Caicos Islands are a British territory in the Caribbean. They're north of Haiti, south of the Bahamas, and east of Cuba. The larger islands of Turks and Caicos are populated, but there are some smaller islands without people.

In 1979, the DEA found out that drug **smugglers** were using one of the unpopulated islands as a transfer point for drugs. The smugglers would land planes on the island to switch drugs to another plane. After getting information about the smugglers' schedule, the DEA set up Operation Boomer/Falcon, which put special agents on the island when a plane was landing. The agents arrested the smugglers and seized the aircraft and thousands of pounds of illegal drugs.

## 1976  Operation Trizo
Using helicopters supplied by the U.S. State Department, Mexican nationals spray plant-killing chemicals on drug fields in Mexico to reduce drug quality.

## 1984  Operation Pipeline
After highway police in multiple states make drug seizures, DEA sets up coordinated highway programs nationwide to seize illegal drugs.

## 1992  Operation Green Ice
DEA creates fake leather goods businesses to catch suspects laundering drug money between Europe and the Caribbean.

## 2003–2005  Operation Jump Start
DEA agents disrupt drug chain that smuggled drugs hidden inside car batteries from Guatemala, through Mexico, and into Texas.

## 2011–2014  Operation Synergy
DEA crack down on designer, or man-made, drugs targeting teens and young adults.

# DEA Air Wing

Sometimes, having agents on the ground isn't enough to solve a case. That's when the DEA Aviation Division comes in. Also known as the Air Wing, the Aviation Division has planes and helicopters that provide ground agents with observations about suspects and can also find and catch suspects. The aircraft can fly so high suspects can't hear them, but agents in the air can spot the suspects.

The Aviation Division is based in Fort Worth, Texas, and has offices all over the world. To become a special agent pilot, candidates—or people who wish to be hired—need at least two years experience as a special agent. They also need to be an experienced pilot. Candidates then undergo a tough training program to achieve the position.

Air Wing started with one plane received from the U.S Air Force in 1971. Today, the Air Wing has over 100 planes and helicopters.

# Intelligence Research Specialists

A special agent position isn't the only career at the DEA. When special agents are in the field, they need to know up-to-date information about their case and their **destinations**. With operations all around the world, the DEA acquires a large amount of information about drug trafficking. Intelligence research specialists receive and review that information to keep special agents one step ahead of traffickers.

Intelligence research specialists bring together the information from law enforcement operations and share it with other people at the DEA or other law enforcement agencies. They gather information, then study and analyze it to make sure it's trustworthy. They also prepare reports for people throughout the DEA and other law enforcement agencies.

# Operation Green Ice

When drug traffickers want to sell drugs, they need a way to make their profit look like it was earned legally. They sometimes set up fake businesses to do so. During Operation Green Ice in 1992, DEA agents posed as leather goods businesses to catch suspects from an international drug-trafficking ring. After they developed the trust of the suspects, the DEA agents arrested them. Nearly 200 suspects were arrested, and the agency seized over $50 million.

Intelligence research specialists must research all the information that's gathered in a DEA operation. This information can be used for other cases or when the case goes to trial.

# Diversion Investigators

Illegal drugs aren't the only drugs people abuse. Prescription drugs are also controlled substances. While many people are prescribed medicines from their doctors, others abuse or steal prescription drugs. Diversion investigators specialize in tracking the supply of prescription medicines. This helps prevent thefts and ensure drugs are **dispensed** legally.

Hospitals, **pharmacies**, and drug companies must follow strict guidelines set by the DEA and the Food and Drug Administration for the dispensing of prescription medicines. Doctors and nurses who write prescriptions and pharmacies that fill prescriptions must register with the DEA. If there's a problem with drugs they prescribe or give—such as missing or ruined drugs—diversion investigators gather information and data to investigate the situation.

Pharmacies must keep track of all the drugs they dispense to customers. The DEA reviews that information to make sure everything is legal.

# Forensic Sciences

To build cases against drug networks and others suspected of illegal drug activity, the DEA must examine mountains of evidence. There are three positions in forensic sciences at the DEA.

New drugs are created all the time, so forensic chemists help the DEA stay current on new illegal drugs sold on the streets. They analyze drugs to find out what they're made of, how they're made, and how strong they are.

DEA forensic science employees have to prepare evidence for trials, and they often have to give **testimony** in trials as well.

Every business uses computers, and the drug business is no different. Forensic computer examiners use advanced methods to access information from drug networks, such as emails. They can even disrupt online exchanges of drugs and money.

The DEA employs fingerprint specialists to match fingerprints on the evidence it seizes to catch the correct suspects.

# Designer Drugs

Designer drugs are chemically created controlled substances made to act like other drugs. For example, forensic chemists analyzed one designer drug made by mixing plant leaves with chemicals to impersonate marijuana. Designer drugs are sometimes sold in normal stores disguised as other products. The people who purchase them know they're actually drugs, but they don't know that the drug could hurt them.

Designer drugs are illegal and can be more harmful than the drugs they're patterned after—even deadly. In 2011, the DEA, along with other local and federal agencies, started Project Synergy to crack down on designer drugs. DEA agents raided stores in the United States selling designer drugs, as well as suppliers in the Middle East and China.

Many designer drugs are advertised as legal. They're given catchy names and marketed to teens and young adults.

# Drug Laboratory Cleanup

Illegal drugs, especially designer drugs, are often processed in illegal laboratories. After the DEA shuts down a drug lab and takes all the necessary evidence, what happens next? The authorities can't throw the contents of the laboratory in the trash because the labs contain many **hazardous** chemicals. They could also contain unclean and unsafe materials and tools, and the drugs themselves may be harmful to the environment.

The DEA, along with the Environmental Protection Agency (EPA) and the U.S. Coast Guard, set up the DEA Clandestine Drug Laboratory Cleanup Program to dispose of the hazardous materials contained in drug labs. This program works with local authorities to ensure that the hazardous materials are disposed of in a way that protects public health and the environment.

# Prescription Drug Disposal

Have you or your family ever had prescription drugs that you didn't need anymore? Old drugs can be dangerous to take. They're also bad for the environment if you throw them away or flush them down the toilet. The DEA operates the National Prescription Drug Take-Back Program. This is a program for people to bring unneeded or old prescription drugs to an authorized disposal center.

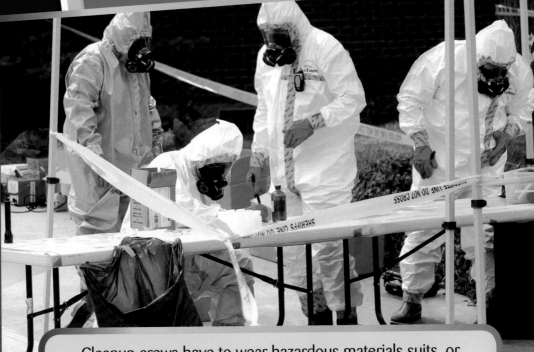

Cleanup crews have to wear hazardous materials suits, or hazmat suits, because drug laboratories use chemicals that are dangerous to the touch.

# Becoming a Special Agent

Not just anyone can become a special agent. To become a special agent, there are many strict requirements. Candidates must be a U.S. citizen between 21 and 36 years old, and they must have graduated college or have experience conducting drug-related criminal investigations. They must also have never been arrested.

Before becoming a special agent, candidates must pass a variety of tests: a written test, a spoken exam, a physical fitness test, a psychological test, and a drug test. These tests make sure their mind and body are healthy and able to undergo challenging and dangerous situations. Special agents need to be in excellent physical condition. The physical test consists of five tasks: push-ups, sit-ups, pull-ups, a 2-mile (3.2 km) run, and a shorter, faster run.

Physical tests are important because being a special agent with the DEA may require a lot of physical work.

After candidates pass their tests, they must undergo 18 weeks of training. They learn about law, writing reports, and recognizing drugs. They undergo firearms training so they know how to use weapons properly.

Candidates in training also have to go through physical training every day. The exercises they do aim to increase their strength, flexibility, and speed. They also learn defense techniques. This will prepare them for a career as a DEA agent.

DEA agents have to work long and sometimes unexpected hours. They sometimes have to relocate to new offices or travel with little notice. The job is challenging and sometimes dangerous, but DEA agents do it to save people, especially young people, from the effects of harmful and illegal drugs.

# Glossary

**abuse:** The mistreatment, misuse, or overuse of something, especially something illegal.

**destination:** The place to which somebody or something is going.

**dispense:** To prepare and give something to someone.

**forensic:** Having to do with the use of science and technology to investigate and establish facts in a court of law.

**hazardous:** Involving risk or danger.

**impersonate:** To pretend to be someone or something else.

**intelligence:** Secret information that a government collects about an enemy or possible enemy.

**money laundering:** Concealing the identity or source of illegally obtained money, often by making it look as if it came from a real business.

**monitor:** To watch carefully.

**pharmacy:** A place where drugs and medicines are sold.

**prescription:** A written direction from a doctor needed for the use of some medicines or drugs.

**prosecute:** To seek punishment for a crime in a court of law.

**smuggler:** Someone who imports or exports goods secretly and illegally.

**testimony:** A statement given under oath, especially in court.

**trafficking:** Buying or selling something illegally.

# Index

# Websites

Due to the changing nature of Internet links, PowerKids Press has developed an online list of websites related to the subject of this book. This site is updated regularly. Please use this link to access the list: www.powerkidslinks.com/fed/dea